Memoirs of a 'Death Cult'

Memoirs of a 'Death Cult'

Warren Sunkar

Copyright © 2024 by Warren Sunkar

The moral right of the author has been asserted. All rights reserved.

No part of this publication may be reproduced, stored in a retrieval system, or transmitted, in any form or by any means, without the prior permission in writing of the publisher, nor be otherwise circulated in any form of binding or cover other than that in which it is published and without a similar condition including this condition being imposed on the subsequent purchaser.

National Library of Australia Cataloguing-in-Publication entry
Creator: Sunkar, Warren, author.
Title: Memoirs of a Death Cult / Warren Sunkar.
ISBN: 9780995371668 (paperback)
ISBN: 9780995371675 (ebook)

First Printing, 2024

DEDICATED TO
KIRK, ALIX AND WOLFY

INTRODUCTION

Somehow and at some time our lives have become almost totally based on the media. Today, we live in a courtroom of public opinion where we are flashed constant headlines and narratives from our televisions and computer screens. In this strange and chaotic world, it seems people will grasp any tool they can to make sense of the reality around them. Perhaps the reason or need for this is that it gives them a personal sense of control or dignity over their short lives by which they are comforted.

However, there are a few of us who have been witness to certain events who know what they have experienced does not coincide with the narratives that other people are given, who watch the mainstream news in incredulity and dismay because the storylines and images the media presents often hide the reality and truth of what really transpired. What adds more to this illusion is that most of society seems content with superficial platitudes and statements which they are given to regurgitate their own 'informed and enlightened' views and perspectives to one another. Maybe in the speed and busyness of our rapidly developing world, people's lives have become too complex to grapple with the underlying causations of events. However, in this struggle to stay 'informed', the paradox is that most people will remain oblivious to the deeper themes and forces that shape their worlds.

After years of working with some of the most experienced and well-respected writers, activists and journalists from around the world, this writer has learned that the assumptions and views of the modern suburbanite who gleans most of their information from the mainstream news are quite erroneous in dealing with the true depths of reality. Let's be frank, in today's surreal and deteriorating social climate expecting any semblance of fact or truth from most mainstream news sources is comparable to going to a butcher for delicate brain surgery. The mainstream media in its mostly blind and aggressive quest to bring you sensationalist headlines is usually very messy and destructive in its methods and fails to ascertain even the simplest of facts. Reporters often create so much social carnage by their very presence that people refuse to share anything deeper or pertinent with them because they lack genuine integrity.

However, it also seems to be an unconscious faculty in most people to simply repeat what they are given from so-called authoritative sources. People do not even consider the damage they might be doing to others and even themselves by potentially spreading gossip and superficial perspectives of events they know very little about. Just because you are told of an event in no way means that you understand what really happened. This is the difference between information and knowledge, and the two can be radically different.

With all this in consideration perhaps it is here that we will begin this tale.

It is about a mystery that this writer literally walked into that had its locus in a small town in Western Australia but its tragic story rippled out over the world. It is about the disappearance of a family and the deaths of a few close friends. The headlines are well known and there is much speculation as to what transpired. The people involved were labelled a 'cult' under the control of a strange enigmatic figure called Simon who groomed people on the internet from all around the world.

After years of tight-lipped silence this writer would like to share with you a deeper story, an unspoken one known only to a few. It is a story very difficult to start because it is something you will not be expecting. As stated in the opening paragraph of this writing, people like to think they have a firm grip on their given reality. As a young man in his late twenties when much of the events of this story transpired this writer's fingers were forced open and what he thought was real changed forever.

For me it is not a question of what to say but how to say it. How do you approach people with a story they might reject as improbable or even ludicrous even though all that is relayed in these pages is of genuine account. There has been no attempt to sensationalise anything but as you read this book you will understand the themes and experiences that are conveyed will underline this very real quandary. These writings may go beyond what you think is acceptable so be prepared to get your brain stretched.

The temperament and vernacular of these writings come from a younger version of myself as I experienced reality in that time period. They are of a young man raised in Australia seeking the deeper answers to life. These writings are more colloquial and less disciplined than my later works. This is done to create a better picture and provide a clearer backdrop for the reader as this writer journeys back a couple of decades.

I have always believed in the responsibility of writers to

bring forth the truth of things even when events may be mired in controversy and confusion. As you will appreciate there is nothing to be gained for this writer in producing this work except a big headache. He would have preferred to stay silent of these things especially in light of the fervent media attention. However, every year some journalist, film producer or writer keeps tracking me down, usually for their own benefit or righteous purpose, and over the years I have become rather tired of it. Sometimes when the past keeps relentlessly knocking on your door you just have to open it.

So, let's set the record straight even if it opens Pandora's Box!

PROLOGUE

Before we dive into the themes and storyline perhaps it is pertinent to give the reader a quick and basic overview of this writer's situation and disposition over the past decade in reference to the crazy situation he found himself in in the aftermath of a media storm.

Let me start this page with a simple question.

Do you actually understand what it is like to be publicly associated with a 'death cult'?

Let me inform you – it is probably one of the hardest labels a person has to live with. In the eyes of society you are completely invalidated and everything you might say or do becomes negatively scrutinised. Family and friends turn their backs on you. It seems that every idiot and A-hole feels they have the right to treat you badly. Anyone who has held a grudge against you thinks it justifiable to spread false gossip and lies about you. If you need assistance from the police they turn their backs thinking you are a criminal. It is also impossible to hold a regular job.

As a well-read young teenager, I was always fascinated with the strange and unexplained. I had read books on various cults such as Jim Jones or the Branch Davidians. You can imagine my own surprise when I turned on my computer one morning to see headlines of myself being associated in a similar context. My online digital signature that had been created mostly on unsubstantiated facts and sensationalist headlines would become a heavy burden.

When you have been at the receiving end of such media attention you quickly realise the world is merciless. You also learn that if you cannot make swift peace with your situation it might just end up destroying you. Another strange experience is that you really begin to see the fears and irrational mechanisms behind civilisation's facade. Humans are a strange mob; one minute they are all hugs and kisses the next minute they are all pitchforks and flaming torches. However, you can find peace knowing yourself as a soul and realising that all that is being attacked is really just the ego. I was lucky enough to have the support of a few good friends to make this rite of passage a little easier.

Fortunately, it was my very experience with said death cult that was to be a gift of patience and endurance in the latter years. Having seen and witnessed events beyond the media circus surrounding the entire debacle, this only made me be more determined to bring certain themes to the surface.

I know there are many unanswered questions in this case that people want answered. To most of those questions I have absolutely no idea as you will realise after reading this work. I can only give account of what I did see and experience at the time. However, what I did witness will probably not present any new insight in regards to the police investigation.

1

MEETING KIRK

This book is a rough chronology of certain events as they transpired. As I'm sure the reader can appreciate, when you are looking back at events that started nearly two decades ago it is not easy to remember exact sequences and timelines. While some memories remain very clear others sometime blur into the kaleidoscope of general remembrance.

This story starts almost two decades ago in the coastal city of Fremantle, Western Australia where my former partner and I were managing a backpacker's hostel. I remember clearly the day I now mention because I was sitting with several backpackers who were all engaged in heated discussion. The tragedy of 9-11 had happened only years before and there were people beginning to ask questions as to what had really happened that fateful day. More people were convinced that there was a lot more going on than what our governments were telling everyone. It was an interesting time as new terms such as 'conspiracy theory', 'illuminati' and 'The New World

Order' were just beginning to surface in discussions amongst travellers. Much of it was still being relayed in hushed tones because in those years there was huge public backlash for even mentioning any of these topics.

Among many backpackers however, these were growing topics of conversation. I remember sitting at a table with my German friend Wolfy (short for Wolfgang) while everyone had a few beers, smoked cigarettes and shared their perspectives on these matters.

There was a young man sitting very quietly at a table and listening very intently. He was a traveller around eighteen years of age who had just arrived from his home in Canada. His hair was dark and very short and he wore glasses. Everyone was debating whether the US government was directly involved in some type of global cover up when I remember him interjecting, saying he definitely believed 9-11 was an inside job, and then we both looked at each other in agreement.

That time was a beautiful period in my life. My partner and I had over the course of a year turned a dingy Fremantle hostel into a thriving backpackers retreat. It was not the usual 'party place' that so many city hostels advertised themselves as being. It was more of an urban getaway where you could meet other travellers in a quiet and safe environment that was very homely. Many people would stay for much longer than they normally would in a typical backpackers, and some of them would make friendships there that would continue for many years after their stay.

As the conversation went on the young man introduced himself as Kirk. He was travelling by himself and came across as a very straightforward and sincere guy. The two of us became friends very easily. In the mornings at the hostel I would sit by myself in the rear courtyard reading various philosophical or metaphysical books. Kirk would sometimes join me. We would sit at the table reading similar themed works and afterwards share or exchange a couple of titles that we found interesting.

I had also published a short work with various spiritual themes written a few years before which I had given Kirk to read. This had sparked his interest and he would ask my opinion on certain esoteric subjects he was reading.

I had not long come back from some more remote places in South-East Asia and I had shared with him some of my strange personal experiences from those travels. I had several quite amazing metaphysical incidents that had me wondering about a lot of things and questioning our reality. When I shared these moments with Kirk he opened up and told me that he too had just recently gone through some sort of transcendent experience which later prompted his travels. It gave us much to talk about!

Over the weeks to come I remember getting into some deep conversations with him. Our friends would often gather around the table mid-morning and sometimes the conversations would continue late into the afternoon. It became very apparent that Kirk, Wolf, myself and others present were all seeking something more from the world than was being presented to us.

Haha...I remember the group was quite the 'liquorice

all-sorts bag' of travellers coming from many different cultures and countries.

As Kirk proved to be a decent and trustworthy person, my partner had given him a part-time cleaning job. He was a very good worker and got along easily with other travellers who were constantly coming and going.

Over those months everyone was having a great time. Kirk sometimes went exploring with other travellers going on adventures down the State's South-West. He appreciated the Western Australian countryside and shared stories of what his life was like in his home on Prince Rupert Island in Canada.

One morning while sitting at the table with a group, Kirk said he had a childhood friend who was going to come over to check out Western Australia. He had told him he was having a good time and wanted his friend to meet me and the rest of the backpacker crew.

Kirk said his name was Alix.

2

Meeting Alix

Most people in our modern world have become so encumbered by the demands and expectations of society in general that few would have the ability to let go of it all and simply follow their inner promptings. For some unknown reason Alix, Kirk and I had no trouble with this. We were dedicated in our search for Truth and it was obvious that we would journey together for a while...

The one great attribute I remember about Alix was his openness to the world. He was a very gentle and free spirit who, like Kirk and myself, was very devoted to unlocking the mysteries of the universe and seeking the deeper truths of reality. Literally, the day he arrived he was already engaging with other travellers in deep philosophical questions and enjoyed sitting in the hostel's back courtyard in deep discussion.

At the time he was reading books on Eastern philosophy. Having been told by Kirk of certain experiences I went through in Myanmar, he asked me lots of questions about my journeys which I shared openly with him. I noticed a nice dynamic between Alix and Kirk, and while Kirk was more reserved and serious in his expression, Alix was much more expressive and flamboyant. Often he would say things people weren't expecting, and sometimes he would bring to the table much unorthodox conversational material – sometimes a little shocking for the unprepared. It was fun.

However, it also became apparent that Alix had an ulterior motive as to why he had come to Western Australia other than to see Kirk and meet me. Only a few days after his arrival, he would take off from the backpackers in the early afternoon and then return later in the evening. He was quiet about where he went and each time he came back he looked a little bewildered and ruffled but also very happy.

After a couple of weeks both Kirk and I noticed this unusual behaviour and asked him about it. He told us he had another friend in Western Australia with whom he had been meeting. Kirk was a little surprised to hear that because he hadn't been told anything about it before. Alix simply said he had made this friend over the internet. We just presumed it might have been a girl.

Then I remember that for a short period Alix stopped going to see his mystery friend. Over the next weeks he spent more time with Kirk, Wolf and the other travellers staying at the hostel. He and Kirk began to explore Fremantle and the surrounding beaches and were having a great time.

However, after a while of roaming around Fremantle with Kirk, Alix had once again started to disappear in the afternoons. I didn't question it but Kirk seemed to be in deeper private discussion with Alix each time he came back. Then one morning at the breakfast table Alix addressed me and Kirk saying that his internet friend, 'Simon', wanted to meet us.

Alix said his friend had already authored a couple of amazing books and this immediately caught my interest. It would be great to meet a more experienced writer. He also said that Simon was perhaps the most extraordinary and in-depth person he had ever met. He even hinted that meeting him would be a somewhat transcendental experience. Both Kirk and I found this strange because Alix was no fool. He was perhaps a little naïve but definitely not stupid.

We just looked at each other saying, "umm, OK…that would be cool."

We couldn't miss an opportunity like that, so we agreed to meet him!

3

Things Get Weird

You can ask any investigator, be it a detective or journalist who has looked into this case, that most of their inquiries have been met with a curious silence in regards to those involved. It is like you are standing on the edge of a cliff throwing rocks into a deep dark chasm. You hear the stones bounce off the walls but you don't hear them hit the bottom. You call out but no one answers you. You peer over the edge but see only darkness.

However, there might be a genuine reason for this. Sometimes it is because the only way you are going to get the full story is to jump off that cliff. It's the only way you are going to understand what is down there. This writer can relay what is down there but he won't, because from where you stand you will only misunderstand me and perhaps even call me a liar.

What I do ask is that you now jump with me. It's the only way you might come to make sense of what I'm about to tell you, or at least understand what is trying to be conveyed by my perspective.

Are you coming?

I don't remember much about the morning Kirk and I drove to Simon's. Alix had given us directions but was not coming with us because Simon had asked specifically to only see us two. It was all very adventurous as we did not know what to expect and I was excited to be meeting another author. However, we were both very curious because Alix seemed to insist that we go even though he still really hadn't told us anything much about Simon. We found that strange.

I recall pulling up in front of a very ordinary house in Cottesloe which was about fifteen minutes away from the hostel in Fremantle. We climbed out of the car and went to the front door. After I knocked a female opened the door and introduced herself as Chantelle, who I quickly surmised was Simon's partner. She led us into the house and picked up a small child playing on the floor who I was later to know as Leela.

Chantelle had a big smile and pointed to the kitchen. She said Simon was in there but she did not join us and went with Leela into an adjoining room. I don't remember much about the house except it was simply furnished with second-hand furniture but I did notice a large poster on the wall of an archangel standing in light over a host of frightened demons. It was a very impressive picture.

We walked into the kitchen and a man, possibly in his mid to late thirties, sat at a table. He was plainly dressed in jeans and a shirt. Looking up at us he smiled, and as we walked into the room he said something I will never forget...

"I'm sorry, I don't really make a good human," was what he said!

I can tell you what went immediately through my mind after hearing his apology. It was very sarcastic! I pictured Alix having a laugh at both myself and Kirk. I was sure he had just sent us here as a practical joke and now we were trapped in a kitchen with some New Age nutter!

Simon continued to talk but after that statement I had just switched off and wasn't really listening. If anyone reading this book has ever been to Fremantle in Western Australia you would understand why. Fremantle has always been an amazing cultural hub of artists, hippies and such but it is also full of many people who had blown a lightbulb by taking way too many drugs. There were so many New Age flakes and crazy spiritual practices in those days. As a writer who wrote on spiritual themes back then, I was constantly being contacted by all sorts of strange people from the 'Freo community' who wanted to meet me. Most of the time it was fun but sometimes it got really weird. I remember once I had a man dressed up in green tights, long pointy shoes and hat, waiting outside my girlfriend's house for hours wanting to talk with me. His mission was to give me a message from the elves. As you can appreciate she had locked the front door and stayed inside.

These things and more flashed through my mind as Simon kept talking. I was thinking playfully…I am so going to get you back for this Alix and when I do I will get you good!

I glanced up at Kirk to see if I could read what was going through his mind as I was sure he was thinking the same thing. But when I looked into his eyes I saw something that blew me away. He was crying. He was also standing very still as he listened intently to what Simon was saying.

I glanced back at Simon sitting at the table who was now studying me. As I focused my attention on him something really strange happened. He stood up and as he did the whole room lit up with this intense spiritual light. It engulfed everything in such a powerful wave of energy that I literally fell to my knees and for a minute or so I felt like purging.

Simon just stood there silent, his whole body glowing.

As the wave of energy was going through us I remember it felt so pure and divine that I felt an immediate sense of deep shame for all of the previous thoughts and presumptions I had just been entertaining, and now I too was crying.

Kirk and myself looked at him open mouthed.

Then Simon said a few things to us which I do not remember and then the wave of energy withdrew.

We were utterly shocked. Then he said, "I'll speak again to you both soon."

The two of us got up to our feet and stumbled to the front door. I remember falling onto the grass outside and lying there for minutes.

Then eventually we got up again, the two of us staggered to the car and climbed inside. I put the keys in the ignition, turned it on and drove off. Once we had turned a corner I pulled the car over to the side of the road. I looked at Kirk who still had tears running down his face and was breathing heavily.

My mouth opened and I just said to him, "W-what was that?"

We looked at each other and then burst into laughter.

After a short time of silence and reflection, I started the car and drove it very slowly back to the hostel.

4

Umm, What Was That...

What do you get when you try to relay a genuine experience that will only clash with a reader's own engendered belief system? You get frustration, disbelief, rejection and sometimes anger.

I'm sure some of you who are presently reading this book are screaming, "BULLSHIT, he is making this up!"

I can also imagine if you are a serious investigator into this case, such as a journalist or police investigator, that you now have resigned me to zero credibility. It's sort of like the story of Jack and the beanstalk – you probably bought this book so that it might give you hard evidence of things that you have subconsciously anticipated in this case and now you think that all I have given you is a handful of magic beans.

But I would ask the reader to put themselves in my shoes and ask the question, what else would you have me say or write if what I say was the reality of what transpired?

Would you have me undermine the truth and validity of

this experience just to succour your ego because it lies outside the parameters of your own experiences?

I also ask you to deeply consider how scary it might be for this writer to share this with so much media attention on this case?

In the introduction of this book I told you all that the only thing this book might give me is a big headache. However, I do ask that if you did decide to jump, that you now see this book through to its end before reaching any conclusion, judgements or psychological assessments.

Yes, I know things have become a little weird but all I can say at this point is that they are about to get even weirder!

When we arrived back at the hostel later that afternoon, Kirk and I went straight to Alix's room. He was sitting there reading as we walked in. We were all very silent and contemplative but you could see in Alix's bright eyes that he was speaking to us mentally saying, 'I warned you to be ready for some next level shiiit!'

I could also see in his eyes that he was relieved because now he had some close friends to talk to about his own similar experiences with Simon. Yet, all he physically did was hand us a couple of books that were next to him and said Simon wanted you to have these. They were books Simon had authored called Servers of The Divine Plan. We took them to read.

After the intense experience we had just gone through I was very determined to understand what had just happened. At that point I was asking myself who or what was Simon?

Throughout the pages of this book this writer will be neither pro nor against Simon. This book is about what Kirk,

Alix and I witnessed and experienced at that time. You will also see that I will not mention the contents of Simon's books unless they should become relevant to this story. If people want to do their own research that is their choice.

Over the next month I was very busy with work but focused what free time I had on reading Simon's book. In those weeks I contacted Simon a couple of times but only on the internet. As I'm sure the reader will understand we all had a lot to process. I think Kirk might have physically visited Simon another time in those weeks but my memory is not so clear about it.

What I do have to say about those few times I did speak to Simon on the internet, is that upon the instant of contact there was a very powerful and beautiful field of living energy that descended upon me each time. At first, due to the intensity of these energies, I found them quite shocking but it all felt very sacred and pure as they lifted my entire being into something infinite and unfathomable. When I questioned him about these energies he called it the field of the Cosmic Christ.

I will say this to the reader, when you are given such a powerful and tangible experience you begin to pay close attention to what is happening. I was very curious about these events and Simon so I launched a barrage of questions at him on the internet.

In his response he shared a little bit of his personal life, that he was from England and that years before he had gone through an extraordinary and instantaneous awakening that occurred near an ancient mound over there.

What he had awoken to was that he was not really human but in essence somewhat insectoid. A non-human avatar which could be conceived as an ultra-terrestrial – a term I hadn't heard before. When I asked him what that meant, he explained it was like some type of inter-dimensional/multi-dimensional being coming from much higher dimensional planes of our universe.

He also mentioned that he (Simon) was a temporary micro-cosm IT was residing in that was rather 'karmically' laden. He told me quite impersonally that his physical vehicle was simply a point of contact with the earth plane and that it would be used to assist the human race as it was going through a critical period of great change. He explained he was a forerunner to much bigger events that were to transpire on Earth.

I was like...say what???

In my rational mind I was like WTF...this dude is crazy! But I then thought, how do I reconcile this with these very real and powerful energies I was receiving? They were so intense and extraordinary. I had experienced them not just once but each time I had contacted him and even that moment while I was on the internet they were washing through me.

Earlier in this book I hinted that I had experienced certain amazing metaphysical energies and exchanges while with Buddhists in the remote areas of Burma. However, this went way beyond that. These energies that he was sharing were so powerful and so engulfing that at some points during the transfer I could not even stand.

The writer in me quickly assessed the situation. So, I'm

talking to a guy who's telling me that he is really like some great cosmic cockroach. I've read his book finding it spiritually very advanced and highly articulate. Each time I have contacted him I have also been completely immersed in a magnificent field of energy.

So, what did I do? I kept asking questions in the hope that something would resolve in me.

So, I asked him, "What is the Cosmic Christ?"

He explained to me that it was a vast field of cosmic intelligence hosting many beings and realities. Then he added, "But its reality is much, much more than that!"

I continued, "So, there are other forms of intelligent life out there in space?"

He replied, "I can tell you this Warren, humans are definitely NOT the most intelligent life in the universe!"

I just thought about the very strange conversation I was having at that moment and went, Oh!

Then another wave of energy hit me.

At that point I didn't know what to think...

5

TIME BENDS WHEN YOU ARE HAVING FUN

Q. What do you realise when you have been selected as first contact for an interdimensional, extra-terrestrial insectoid species?

A. That life goes on except now you have a lot more shit to think about!

A few months later I was settling into a new house in the South-West town of Balingup. I had been working at the backpackers for well over a year and I had grown tired of all the urban craziness and lack of sleep that came with the job. It was great to be out of the city and have time to research everything I could about ETs, UFOs, conspiracy, ancient civilisations, spiritual philosophy and whatever else that went with the territory. I found there was a lot to learn!

Kirk and Alix were still with me at that time and Wolfy would come down on his breaks from working on a mission with indigenous children in the State's north. My partner had stayed in Fremantle working but was hoping to join us all in a few months.

Over several months of 'backpacking' Kirk had become quite proficient on the guitar, and Alix was also constantly practising so whenever we had time we would grab a few instruments and go play in a nearby park. Balingup was a small town and we were having a really nice time meeting some of the locals who would sometimes come over to the park with their instruments and play with us. I had not been in contact with Simon since those times in Fremantle but I was deeply pondering his writings. Kirk and Alix had only limited contact with him at that time but informed me that Simon had set up an internet forum that was for seekers of truth around the world.

At this point in the story I would like to share with readers something they might find interesting. From those few times I had contacted Simon and there had been those beautiful exchanges of energies, I began to realise that somehow they had changed me. It was like my consciousness had been uplifted and cleaned. My dreams had become way more lucid. I was more acutely aware of my surroundings and even displayed certain psychic capacity. I knew that both Kirk and Alix were going through the same thing. We also felt more impersonal to things in a good way and would often have spontaneous moments of deep connection with the Earth and Life around us. This was evoking within us some new sensations and feelings. We were also experiencing touches of higher dimensional realities as if some veil had come off – a sort of sight beyond sight that would come and go intermittently. The entire sensation left you not really caring about the dramas and troubles of worldly life, almost as though they were somewhat unimportant and curiously far away.

I think it was around that time that Wolfy could have had a few moments when he thought we might have been smoking some sort of happy weed (Wolf had never met Simon or at that time even read his books,) but we hadn't.

More weeks flew past and soon it was time for Kirk and Alix to go back to Canada. I was sad because we'd had such an unforgettable time together but they also told me they would be back. Alix then relayed he had heard from Simon and that he and his family were living in a country town called Nannup not far away. I laughed because it was a town literally next door to where I now lived. It was an interesting coincidence!

Both of them said they would be joining Simon's internet forum but I told them at that point I had no inclination to join. I felt strongly that I had to contemplate and adjust to the strange reality shift I was experiencing, however I did tell them I would stay in touch.

More months went by and Wolfy and I were working on the house. I was loving the countryside and was making a lot of new friends. We were also having some fun times exploring the area and going to a few local parties. The days went by quickly.

Over the next months I heard from Kirk and Alix only occasionally. What they did tell me was they were finding it very hard adjusting back to their old lives. I understood what they meant. Things had changed for me as well. Energetically I felt very different and I was perceiving reality beyond the five senses. I had also become more inwardly quiet. I sometimes tried to share these experiences with a few friends but quickly understood that it was all too 'out of the box' for them.

I would have the reader understand that the consciousness shift I was experiencing was not in any way dissociative or some type of psychic illusion but coherent waves of transcendent insight that were coming from planes beyond the physical. It did not seem supernatural but very natural, as if some forgotten inherent faculty was now being restored. It was very different to what is sometimes referred to as a 'psychic state'. I can only describe it as a deep awakening of soul consciousness.

Then one day I was unexpectedly contacted on the phone by a friend I knew in the nearby town of Nannup. He told me he had to go to the city for a few days and asked me if I could look after his house from which he was running his small business. I said no worries. I hadn't visited Nannup for quite a while and I loved the area. I thought it would be nice to take a break from all the gardening I was doing at that time.

Coincidently, that afternoon I also received an email from Simon from whom I hadn't heard for a while. He asked if he could see me soon as he said he had something to ask of me. I told him his timing was a cool synchronicity because I had just been asked to go to Nannup the very next day. We arranged to meet at my friend's house that next morning.

6

A REALITY OVERHAUL

I will always remember that day when Simon came over. Of all the memories I have of that time it is perhaps the clearest. It is also the day I most loathe to share because of people's possible reactions. I said before that almost everyone wants to hear things that validates their own experiences and concepts of reality. Over many hard earnt years of experience, I have learnt that people will usually and often harshly reject anyone or anything that conflicts with their own ideals, assumptions and beliefs floating around in their little ego bubble of reality.

But here I ask the reader; if that is all humanity does, how do we expect to really learn anything? Perhaps this is one of the reasons why most of the race just seems to go around and around, in a violent and repetitive history of useless loops and circles...

Let's get things straight here, I'm not judging anyone. For most of my younger life I had been doing the same.

However, about this day, all I can say for me personally is POP!

As Simon walked through the back door of my friend's house that morning I hadn't realised how tall he actually was. As he shook my hand and said hello I realised his hands were much bigger than mine. Perhaps it's a curious way to start this chapter but one thing I do want to share with readers is I found he was a kind and very gentle man.

I know that after all the later media fanfare people would expect someone evil or insidious. I'm just saying I found him a nice guy and I liked him.

I also know that some people stepped forward after his disappearance to present a different picture but I know humans can be complex. What I mean by this is people often want demons, and use scapegoats for issues they don't want to confront in themselves. I also said in the introduction of this story that once you have been pinned with a label such as 'death cult', anyone with a grudge feels it's their right to say anything they want about you. However, I can plainly see that what a lot of people pitch as the truth is usually not the complete story.

Simon had brought a few preservative-free beers for us to share as we sat down and talked.

He had come to ask me if I could help him with some money to publish one of his new books. Simon had written about five different books and many articles over the years, most of which today remain unpublished. He was asking me to help with funding a new one.

I said, "Sure." Being a writer myself, I knew how hard it

was to get money to produce independent books. Although I didn't have much money at that time, because of the high quality and content of his writings, I said I would help in any way I could. I was also really impressed by the volume of works he had produced and so I asked him how he survived.

He said he was on health care for an injured back that was giving him a lot of trouble. He lived fortnight to fortnight on the pension. I told him I was rather surprised the government would give him health care for just a bad back because it was very hard to get government assistance for anything.

He told me when he went to a job services interview with the government employment agency (Centrelink) a few months before, the lady interviewing him had asked him about his future employment prospects. He said he felt it better he be honest with her and told her he was an inter-cosmic traveller from other far regions of the universe who had come to assist humanity on a very specialised mission! He then said that when she realised he was speaking seriously to her she just quickly ticked a box that said he was unemployable, gave him a few forms to sign and then speedily sent him away.

I had to laugh at that one!

After that, we talked a bit more blah and then went on to talk a bit more on certain world topics which I will not go into here. However, at a certain point in this conversation I began to feel an energy building in the room and in a very short while it was growing much stronger in intensity. This time, however, I did not feel a purgative effect but only a sense of what I could call Eternal Love. The waves of energy kept coming and with my 'sight' I could see a dark electrical field open around Simon. I can only describe this space as dark matter.

It was then something even more interesting happened. I watched a large arc of plasma open up above him which then began to descend down on us. The space around us turned into a flashing sequence of multi-coloured lights. I looked at Simon and then I saw IT!

At first what I observed was what looked like a few long glowing legs that opened the space above us like someone was drawing back a curtain. IT then began to partially descend from metres above Simon's head and looked like some bio-luminescent insect. At this point I would like to add that during this whole experience I did not feel threatened in any way, quite the opposite – I felt a deep sense of peace, love and what could be called sacred appreciation.

However, what was also becoming clear, that what I was seeing of this creature was only partial. This great being had only put a little part of itself through the interdimensional vortex above us. I could sense that its full form was much bigger and grander than what I was presently seeing.

I looked at Simon and his physical form had gone somewhat limp, like some dangly thing underneath IT. That does not mean IT was using him as some sort of puppet because what I could see was that in essence, Simon was this creature. At least at the core of his being he was intrinsic to its energetic bio-field, like some form of extension.

It was no longer Simon as a personality that was talking to me but this great cosmic being that was speaking through him. In this energetic space we continued to converse but

I do not remember much about this because we were no longer using physical speech. The whole experience was very multidimensional and the communication went well beyond the five senses. As you might appreciate, such an experience is hard to translate. Most of what can be remembered relates as more of a feeling and an energetic imprint that is left on one's being.

As for how long this all went on for it is hard for me to say as linear time was sort of thrown out the window. However, when the being and its presence began to withdraw, it was still morning. Then after the energies had left we both just sat there for a short while. Simon was silent and just watching me with a smile. I was feeling elated by the whole experience.

He then said it was now time for him to go.

I just smiled as there was little to say except that I would help him fund his new book.

With that he left.

I then just sat there by myself on the couch for a couple of hours.

My mind had drifted out into the cosmos contemplating all of the worlds and beings possibly 'out there'.

Then as I watched a small bug scuttle over the floorboards near my feet, I also knew I was going to be much, much kinder to insects!

7

BECOMING YOUR OWN
X-FILE

Over the years I have had many people demanding explanations regarding this case.

What I have to say to all those people who were around at that time is…were you really listening?

At that time we were trying to tell people our experiences but all we were met with was strange looks, disbelief and closed doors. We quickly learnt that most people, including loved ones and family, will only see you as weird or possibly taking hard drugs.

We started to realise we were by ourselves and a form of withdrawal was needed.

A necessary fence goes up because you are now dealing with subject matter that most people have no way of incorporating into their reality. We also understood that most of society is too emotionally and mentally immature to deal with a topic such as extraterrestrials.

I am sure there are those reading this book who are laughing at or rejecting this work based on these topics and who will try very hard to psychoanalyse and disprove what I am saying. This is only because extraterrestrials lie outside their own conclusions of possibility.

They are just proving my point!

More months went by...

Over that period I shared very little contact with Simon except for a few emails. I had sent him some money for the publishing of his new book and was reading some of his new works.

Kirk and Alix continued to contact me. They told me they were on the internet forum that Simon had set up. They would send me a few of the articles they were sharing online. Most of them were spiritual, conspiracy or science based. They said they would be back in Western Australia soon and asked to stay with me. I told them they would be welcome.

During this time I was going through a deep personal catharsis. What I will share with readers is that when you have been presented with a set of experiences that are far outside the parameters of what you have assumed as reality, they will eventually change you. At the time you don't really understand what is happening but then one day you simply wake up and realise you are different. What you once perceived of as 'life' had now opened into realms of greater possibility, and what used to be 'the world' had somehow become much smaller. Trying to engage with it was like putting on a ridiculously small set of old childhood shoes, your toes would barely fit in.

I would sit and listen to my friends and family but what they talked about was so out of context with what I had been experiencing that it seemed no longer that important. I would try to be attentive as they talked about birthdays, their jobs and Christmas but I was somewhere else entirely. I was thinking about God, other worlds and aliens. I knew that Kirk and Alix were going through the same.

So, I just let everyone fall away.

I could not share a purposeful relationship with my partner. That also went for my family and some of my friends because I would often try to share a different context of reality but they would just sort of tune out. It had nothing to do with not loving them – it was more that you had nothing really in common with them anymore. It wasn't a bad thing. It had more to do with consciousness growth, and I was now in an inner space where I had nothing to really offer them.

I would watch my partner and some of my friends try to grapple with these changes. I realised I could no longer give them what they wanted and this was hurting them. It was better to withdraw for their sake.

Now a person might scream out at this point and say this all proves I was in some weird alien cult.

To that I would say, "No moron...think about it!"

The only thing happening at that time was that we had been exposed to a set of very peculiar experiences which we had no choice but to investigate thoroughly, to make a deeper sense of things. It is what you do when you are faced with the seemingly inexplicable.

As for the changes we were going through, they were

an organic and sympathetic response to the new stimuli and information we were being inundated with. As I have said before...put yourself in our shoes and consider these things from our perspectives.

Anyway, after several months of being back home in Canada, Kirk and Alix came back to Western Australia to stay with me back in Balingup for a short while.

8

YOU CAN'T UNSEE WHAT YOU HAVE SEEN

What had become apparent to us was that humanity understands very little about the true nature of consciousness. Humans have, as a natural organic ability, the means to interact with many different spectrums and fields of reality. However, in most humans these faculties are dormant and are somewhat inaccessible. I would have the reader ponder how and why this could have happened?

I will also add that should these latent faculties be turned back on there are some powerful revelations to be had as to how humanity is presently living – and they are not kind. We as a race really need to grow up spiritually and take more responsibility over our lives because modern 'life' is killing us.

It was good to see Kirk and Alix again. They both relayed their adventures from the last several months. The lives of the three of us had gone on an unexpected tangent and it was good to share these things with each other.

They also told me they were on the internet forum more these days interacting with other seekers of knowledge who had now formed an inner group.

The energy that Simon had shared with us many months ago had somehow changed us fundamentally. The three of us were having all sorts of spiritual experiences and psychic phenomena happening to us. Over time we had become much more resonant with Life and this was bringing these multidimensional experiences to us. It was like some sort of benign consciousness upgrade.

However, we also became aware that this presented some other problems. We had become very sensitive to things. The loud noises of urban living, the smells of synthetic perfumes and chemicals seemed to almost hurt us. We could see more deeply how 'modern life' was so negatively impacting humanity on many levels.

What was stranger is that we could also see various spirits possessing people at times and this made us a little wary. Some of these beings knew we could see them and could become troublesome or even hostile. We realised that most people have no idea they are often being used and influenced by these realities. It was all new and very strange.

I could only guess as to what Simon had been experiencing all those years as the energies he was subjected to were much more powerful.

I won't share with the reader all these experiences but you can imagine that being in such a sustained open state had you considering the world very differently. Again, I would point out that this was in no way an alternate state of consciousness but was an initiated state of expanded consciousness 'being'. There is a very big difference.

For the next few months we spent a lot of time in nature. We would often go hiking through the forest because nature seemed to comfort us. The times we did spend at the house we worked on music and wrote poetry. We had also returned to playing music in the local park where a few local friends would come down and sometimes join us.

I had told Kirk and Alix about my last experience with Simon and they shared similar stories.

They also introduced me to some people online who were on the forum and who were sharing various insights and spiritual experiences from around the world. Everyone on the forum seemed to be seeking something deeper and they were all very benevolent people. I only went online a few times to read and share a few things but in terms of inquiry I kept it very light. Simon seemed to be always present online and sharing his own writings. I spoke again with him a few more times on the internet in those months and each time I did there was always a very powerful energy present in the exchange.

During that period I knew that Kirk and Alix visited Simon a few times as he lived in the nearby town of Nannup. They told me Simon mostly discouraged any personal visits or contact because – get this – he did not want the group to be perceived as any sort of cult. He desired an impersonal online forum where people could share their experiences and insights as they sought truth and explored deeper concepts.

They were also quiet about any experiences they might have had while visiting him those few times.

The months with them went by quickly. We were having a great time being ourselves, exploring and having fun. Though we would keep contact over the next few years it would be the last time I would see them alive. These are cherished memories.

9

CUTTING LOOSE

Sometimes, when you are going through deep inner changes your outer life shifts as well. All change implies inner deaths but also catharsis. When things have been easy we often resist that change but I knew that to fight it would only bring greater suffering.

Life was calling me to step up and I realised I had to follow...

With Kirk and Alix gone back to Canada I had some deep thinking to do in regards to my personal life. I was no longer the same person and it was futile trying to act otherwise. There was no way I could be content in resolving myself to any material disposition or normalised function. I had glimpsed beyond the veil and there was to be no turning back for me now. To do so would only be contrary and resistant to what I felt within my heart. I needed to know more, to seek deeper truths and understand the universe and God – but I realised it would come at a price.

Now I don't want to bore the readers too much with my personal life so I will get through this chapter quickly.

A few weeks after Kirk and Alix had left I had a very lucid dream...

I was walking side by side with my partner down a long road. We walked to a junction where a path splintered off to the right. At that point I came to a stop and looked down to see a backpack at my feet. My partner had continued walking straight ahead, and as I stared after her I could see she was wearing a wedding dress. A male figure was walking next to her. I was a little saddened by this but knew what I was being called to do. So I picked up my backpack and just started walking down the other pathway not turning back.

The message was simple. Over the next few weeks I said goodbye to her and my family. I would have a bit of money after the split so I decided I would travel. I needed some time to process and then think about starting my life afresh.

This was not easy. Everything was to be left behind and I knew I must do it quick, sort of like ripping off a band-aid. The pain would be short and sharp but better for everyone in the long term. I gave away some of my money to a few friends who needed it and left behind all of my possessions. With the remainder of the money I bought some tickets and took off to South-East Asia.

After I arrived in Thailand I just wanted to forget everything for a while so I spent most of the first couple of months with other travellers, drinking and partying. I cut really loose for a short while. My friend Wolfy had come over and joined me for a short time and probably thought I had gone off the rails a bit.

However, the pain I felt was more than just leaving my friends and family. I realised that with my chosen pathway I would now be quite lonely. Not because of a lack of people around me but because I knew and understood that reality was not what most people perceive it to be. I knew this insight could not be shared with anyone as it would only weird them out or confuse them. Especially with society being what it was.

Now when I look back at that time, it was a rite of passage and my drinking nothing but an immature reprieve from what I would eventually have to face within myself. I knew then that other ET life forms existed and were interfacing with our own planet. I was determined to know more.

Anyway, no matter what spin I might now put on it, I did party pretty hard for that short period.

Eventually, I found a sanctuary in one of the small islands off the coast of Thailand. I had to make peace with my choices as well as with myself. I enjoyed a simple time there for just over a month but as my money ran out, I knew I would have to go back to Australia.

I had no plans or clue as to where I would go or what I would do when I got there.

Then one morning I turned on my laptop.

I had been emailed by my friend who asked if I could look after his business again but this time for a week. I decided that Nannup was where I had to go and then figure out the next stages of my journey.

10

MEETING TONY

The day I returned to Western Australia I caught a bus straight to Nannup. It was a long journey taking several hours and I was very tired and jet lagged. Hopping off the bus I walked directly to my friend's house who was making final preparations to leave early the next morning. After I arrived and caught up with him, he let me freshen up and then he showed me what needed to be done around the house while he was gone. As I had already looked after his house I knew basically what to do. He also told me he had a new gardener who would be working there in the mornings.

After that I remember just walking to my room and crashing.

When I awoke my friend was pretty much out the door and saying goodbye. He said he would see me in a week. He also told me the gardener was out the back working and I should go say hello as he was a nice guy. Then he left.

I went into the kitchen, made myself some breakfast and

walked out to the side veranda of the house to eat my cereal. A man in his early thirties had seen me come outside and walked up to say hello. He said his name was Tony and I replied with a hello and then introduced myself. However, he said he already knew of me as Simon had spoken of me before. (I had no idea that he was living with Simon and Chantelle.)

I laughed at the coincidence of meeting him as I had literally just arrived in town.

We sat down for a short time to talk. I could very easily see that Tony was a gentle and humorous person but I could also see a little of a wild side. He was openly gay or bi and I quickly guessed that he was in an open relationship with both Chantelle and Simon. He didn't hide it and you could also tell that he loved Leela who was Simon and Chantelle's daughter. Knowing they were all very quiet and private people I didn't pry.

Like me, he wasn't on the internet forum much preferring to spend most of his time gardening for extra cash. Our conversation widened as we talked a little on a few esoteric subjects and shared perspectives on what was happening in the world at that time. Many people were seeing that the world leaders were war mongers and this had everyone thinking of the future state of world affairs. However, we were both appreciative to be in the little South-West town of Nannup seemingly far away from all the crazy world events going on.

He said he liked being in the countryside because he could avoid crowds of people. He told me he was very psychically sensitive to nature and liked being outdoors. I guessed that staying in constant close proximity to Simon would have greatly enhanced certain senses of higher awareness in him and he told me this was so.

Then after that short talk Tony stood up and told me he would see me around. He then went back to do some more gardening.

11

MY THIRD MEETING WITH SIMON

Over the next few months I spent some time getting to know the local community. I was lucky to have an artist friend who had kindly offered a caravan at the rear of his house for me to stay in.

At that time I had decided to get back into writing. I was also spending a lot of time researching and delving into all sorts of topics. I had amassed quite a collection of writings on spirituality and conspiracy as well as some more obscure ancient texts.

My friend who was also into these things would call me up for a coffee in the afternoons where we would sit together at his kitchen table. I would light a cigarette and often he would roll a joint for himself as we discussed many esoteric themes.

I was aware that both Chantelle and Tony were working at jobs around town but I rarely spotted them. When we did occasionally bump into one another we would exchange a simple hello and that was all. I knew they had a house somewhere out of town but did not know where it was. I never saw Simon in town because he hardly ever left his house. He told me once the reason for this was that if certain energies were coming through him they could destabilise people, and if they were possessed they might even attack him. As I had felt these energies and considered what they could do, I didn't question him further on this.

Over those months I had very little contact with Kirk and Alix. They would sporadically send me a rare catch-up email to let me know what they were doing but it seemed they were online a lot more with the inner group that had been set up on the Truth Fellowship/Gateway forum.

One day, very early in the morning, I went for a walk through the quiet streets of Nannup. There were only a couple of people who were out and about. As I walked down the main street I heard my name being called from further down the road and when I looked up I saw Simon and Tony.

They were standing behind their parked car and Simon was just saying goodbye to Tony who waved at me but then started to walk in the opposite direction. It looked like he was going to work somewhere.

Simon began walking towards me to say hello. Immediately I felt the presence of his energy field and as he came closer his aura seemed to glow brighter in an ethereal but clearly visible, white light.

On the side of the road about twenty metres behind me stood a delivery truck driver and another local who were busily talking away. Suddenly, they came to an abrupt stop in their conversation and turned around to face Simon.

He walked up to me and shook my hand. By that time the energetic field had become so powerful I thought I was going to drop then and there. I was able to stay on my feet and just let the energy work its way through me. Behind me however, one of the men had fallen to his knees with tears running down his face. But the delivery truck driver just stood there, absolutely frozen and looking petrified.

The transmission of these energies continued for a few minutes. It is hard to remember exactly for how long because in these moments time seemed to bend and waver but I was totally aware that these energies were healing me on many levels of my being.

Then Simon and I walked over to where the two men were. One was still on his knees crying; the other looked very desperate and afraid. I felt at that moment he was either about to flee or charge at us in blind desperation. Simon had sensed this as well and began to instantly withdraw the energies. We then turned and walked away from the pair.

From the other side of the road I watched them regain their composure. The man who had fallen on his knees stood back up. Then a most interesting thing happened. The two men just resumed talking and laughing as though nothing had happened. They were barely aware of us.

I turned to Simon who seemed to have read my mind and he said, "Some people are just too asleep in this matrix…they won't remember a thing."

That had me deeply thinking about the nature of reality!

Then we continued to chat for a few minutes on more mundane things. Eventually we said goodbye to one another and went our own ways.

12

WHEN THINGS GO WRONG

Life is strange in that one day you can be lying in an open field, gazing out into the infinite sky and pondering the magnificence of the universe, then later that same day you get hit by a truck.

Several months had gone by since that last contact with Simon. I was still living in my friend's caravan and was doing a lot of creative writing. I never saw Simon, Chantelle or Tony during that period, not even casually around town.

I had made many friends in Nannup and was having a great time. Little did I know that things were soon going to change.

Kirk and Alix were still online connecting with other people from around the world on the Gateway forum. They had continued to send me various articles and posts which I read and often responded to. The forum was highly impersonal and a space where people would share a lot of cutting-edge information on many diverse subjects. Everyone on it seemed earnest and sincere. They were reading not only

Simon's work but sharing the works of many other writers, speakers, scientists and spiritualists both modern and ancient from around the world. It was also presenting a lot of information that exposed hidden corruption and darker unseen elements in governments and other places.

So Simon was gathering people from all around the world onto a single platform to share this information. I ask the reader – what could go wrong?

One night I was violently awoken from my sleep. I was gasping for air because it felt like someone was choking me. I opened my eyes to see a black shadow-like form sitting on my stomach with its hands around my throat.

You could not imagine what was going through my mind as it was happening. I was terrified.

This thing looked demonic and its energy felt very dark. I was struggling to breathe and for minutes I writhed and turned in panic trying to fight it off. I felt this just might be my end and I was going to die. At that point I can remember thinking that if anyone was to find my body the next morning they would probably just assume I choked in my sleep or had a heart attack.

As the air left my lungs I shut my eyes. I said a prayer and then at that very moment I felt a surge of divine energy come from above. It was like blue electricity which tore through the room and blew this shadow creature back to where it came from.

For a time I lay there quietly trying to regain my composure. It had all happened very quickly. I eventually sat up but as I was still quite shaken I kept praying until the sun came up.

Confused from the night's events, I sat there in the caravan wondering what was going on. It was very early and most people were still in bed so I decided to go for a walk and pull myself together.

As I walked through the quiet country streets I turned towards a local park. It was then I felt as if something was wrong and began to feel giddy and disoriented. Suddenly a large wave of putrid energy seemed to hit me. It felt as if someone had just thrown petrol on me and had lit a match. I hit the ground burning with such an intense pain that it made me feel like vomiting. This black fire seemed to stick to me like some tenebrous goo and I laid there and cried for a while in utter desperation.

I was stuck on the ground for several minutes but somehow I climbed to my feet and staggered back to my friend's house. I slipped through the back gate into the caravan where I collapsed heavily onto the bed. I lay there crying and, at some points, silently screaming because of the pain.

I was utterly exhausted and felt like I wanted to die.

My friend came down to the caravan later that day because he hadn't seen me. I just croaked to him that it appeared that I had severe food poisoning. He said he hoped I would get better and later that evening brought me a small plate of food.

All this continued in waves for a few days. Most of the time I suffered quietly and only got up occasionally to go to the toilet.

After the third day the pain began to subside enabling me

to gain some semblance of functionality. I hid how bad I was really feeling from my friend. He could see I was quite ill and had brought me a few meals over the three days. I couldn't eat them but I was appreciative for his care.

On the third day I had decided to get on my laptop. I wanted to contact Simon, Kirk or Alix to let them know what had been happening. I was still feeling awful.

I quickly discovered that Kirk and Alix had been hit in Canada as well. Alix told me that Kirk had collapsed and that he had to carry him to his bed. They had emailed Simon who had also been taken severely ill and who had told them this was a hit from dark forces. He had told them he had been through this before but also said this was more intense than what he had experienced the other times it had happened to him. He was calling the dark energy Tenebrae. I knew what he meant because it seemed to cling to you and sort of rape you of your vital energy.

I then realised we were all under some metaphysical attack. Somehow and for some reason we had pissed something off, and whatever it was wanted us out of commission.

13

THE ATTACKS CONTINUE

We live in a play within a greater play of forces which most of humanity knows nothing about.

What I did not understand at that time was that the attacks I had just experienced would become a long test of endurance. Throughout the next year I would go through several more, though none as intense as that first one.

I had comprehended that the work and collaboration of the group forum had triggered a hostile response from certain perfidious intelligences that usually remain hidden. However, they were attacking not just the online inner group but anyone who was connected to any people involved.

The energetic changes I had gone through, as amazing as they were, had become a curse. I had become much more sensitive to certain frequencies that were enabling me to see and experience a much wider range of consciousness and energetic realities but this change also had me more open to certain perfidious energies that exist in other dimensions.

We live in a world that is ignorant of other consciousness spectrums. We exist in a vast sea of energies and whether people wish to believe it or not, there are other realities and beings that work against humanity from different planes of existence. Their objective is to keep humanity locked into five-sense reality as their own existence relies on human ignorance. They do not like it when people are able to ascertain or see them and will attack those who threaten them with any form of exposure.

People also do not understand that we are being constantly bombarded with certain frequencies intent on harming us. Some of these are demonic, some are man-made and others are from off-world origins which I will mention little of in these writings. Over a decade ago, as you can imagine, you could not talk about these things to anyone as they would only shut you down as idiotic. However, I now mention these things because it seems a lot more people are now able to hear and understand these things.

Over that year Kirk and Alix were having the same problems and revelations in Canada. They would communicate to me their own experiences. They also told me that others who were on the forum were going through these things and being constantly targeted. I had not seen or contacted Simon in many months but they told me he was being completely overwhelmed by these attacks.

They also informed me that the being that was with Simon had now withdrawn. I didn't like the sound of that.

One thing I did realise during that time is that no matter what you might be going through, no matter how hard or terrible it is, the world keeps going. You are required to endure and function through whatever might be happening – and that is what I did. Over that period I found that keeping myself busy and distracted in more mundane tasks really helped, so I took on a few jobs and hung out with my local friends. It made the time more bearable.

However, now I could see that these attacks weren't just affecting me. People in town were now saying they were feeling extremely tired and just plain exhausted. They were attributing it to a variety of factors but I could see that these energies were affecting larger areas. I could see some of these energies were having a vampiric effect on people's energy fields, keeping them tired and shut down.

14

MY FOURTH MEETING WITH SIMON

As months went by I struggled through this difficult time. I took up a few jobs and quit writing for a while. Eventually, I found myself in a new relationship and I was spending time with my partner doing relationship things...

One morning I bumped into Chantelle who was working somewhere in town. She asked me if I could help Simon to replenish a couple of gas bottles for their hot water system. She told me Simon's back was really bad, and Tony, who would normally help, was away in Perth for a few months.

She wrote down their phone number and address as I still had no clue as to where they actually lived. I said I would call her in a couple of days to organise the bottles.

We then talked briefly and Chantelle told me she was also being metaphysically attacked and was exhausted. She said Simon had fallen ill through it all and she seemed quite desperate. She said the attacks at their house had been unrelenting.

I said I would see them in a couple of days.

I don't remember much about the drive to Simon and Chantelle's house other than it was a few kilometres out of town and semi-remote. As I drove towards the house I saw it was just an old and simple farmhouse on one of the local's properties. That's all I can recall.

I had phoned them to let them know I was coming and Simon was already outside waiting expectantly. When I pulled the car up close to the house both Chantelle and Leela came outside to say hello. I changed the gas bottles, doing most of the lifting myself as I could plainly see that Simon was not well. He looked quite haggard and said his back was hurting him.

Then after I had fitted one of the gas bottles and lifted the empty one onto the back of the ute they invited me in for a cup of tea. As we walked to the house he apologised that the energies in the house were bad. He said he was being targeted by groups of off-world beings that I would later come to know as Greys.

As we all walked into the house together I was very shocked to feel an intense and quite sickening energy permeating the entire house. It felt like some abhorrent artificial frequency that was being transmitted through all the rooms. I wanted to get out of there immediately.

Simon was looking pale and worn down. Chantelle passed me a cuppa and we all walked outside. He said things had gone wrong with his mission on Earth. I was still reeling from the energies inside the house and could only look at him sympathetically. He seemed quite helpless. As I looked at the family they all seemed to be struggling.

Having shared what they were going through over the past several months I knew this was no delusion. In such a situation it's not like you can call the police and say, 'Hey, I'm being attacked by aliens can you please send in the army?'

Well you could but the van that would rock up would be a white one!

There was not much I could do but I asked if I could assist with anything else. He just smiled and said that it would probably get better soon. Then after the tea and talk I gave Chantelle a hug and said goodbye. I said I would probably catch them in town and if they needed any help to just ask.

15

MANGOES, COCONUTS AND BEACHES...

Over the next few months I didn't hear anything from Simon or Chantelle. I hadn't seen them in town but was aware that Tony had been seen. I was only rarely contacted by Kirk and Alix but when I was, they told me they were still struggling very heavily with multiple metaphysical attacks. They let me know they were still in constant contact with Simon who was now quite desperate. He had been smoking marijuana and was now taking pain killers and other forms of medication to try to relieve what he was going through. He had also been looking at various medicines from South America to see if they could assist him.

At that time my relationship with my new partner was going well. I still kept myself very busy with work because if I even tried to meditate or anything of the sort I would be attacked again. Doing menial things resulted in being attacked a lot less so I was doing them happily.

However, what I did need to do was process. The last few years had been incredible and I was still coming to terms with many things. I had been thrust into a strange new world of heightened consciousness reality. As exciting as it was, I had quickly found that it could be very difficult in a world that was still quite asleep to many things. I still had so many questions, and all these events made me wonder what is really going on 'out there'. I had been just a kid from the Perth suburbs but now I had to find a way to reconcile these incredible energetic and consciousness changes.

I knew I needed a break. I decided I would go back to Thailand to be by myself, not to party but to sit, think and perhaps write for a month or two.

I had saved some money from my caring job and so I jetted off. It was the off-peak tourist season and so I easily found a nice place to relax in seclusion. In a small thatched hut on a remote beach, I was eating mangoes, drinking coconut water and thinking about my life over the past several years.

Having bought a small laptop I began writing some of my experiences down. I had also decided to take up smoking again, (I had always enjoyed it, especially when writing) and it was nice to just lay out in a hammock in the sun.

Then one morning I had a very beautiful experience...

I had just made myself a coffee and was about to sit down in front of my computer when I felt a beautiful energy start to gently cascade from above. It slowly began to grow in power as a field of light that wrapped around my entire body like a warm cocoon. It reminded me of the energies that Simon had once shared with me.

I stilled and allowed this light to saturate my entire being as my physical body began to lightly pulsate in response to what was happening. I then heard a very gentle omniscient voice that seemed to come from everywhere and nowhere.

The voice told me that soon things would change and I would be on my own. It told me not to worry because everything was fine. I didn't know what it meant but knew to trust it. It told me I would be witness to things, that I should keep writing and remember everything. I then felt another surge of energy while this omniscient presence withdrew. I spent that entire morning in a totally blissed out state.

I thoroughly enjoyed the next couple of weeks by myself.

What was really cool was these angelic energies had lifted any remaining dark energies that had clung to me from the attacks over the past months, which on some level had still been affecting me. I was feeling good again. Very good!

16

A KNOCK ON THE DOOR

It was months later and I was sitting on the rear veranda with my partner having a cigarette, (I had been failing hopelessly in trying to kick the habit since I came back from Thailand), when I heard a knock on the front door. I stood up and went to answer it. As I opened the door I was very surprised by who was there. It was Simon. He was standing there with a medium sized box under his arm.

Saying 'hello', he walked in and put the box on the kitchen bench. I then led him outside where I introduced him to my partner. He looked a lot better than when I had last seen him.

After a brief introduction my partner got up and went to the kitchen to make us both a coffee leaving us alone to talk for a bit. I told Simon how surprised I was to see him and he just laughed.

He then told me he was dissolving the online forum. He said the attacks had become so bad over the past months that he had felt like ending his life. However, he also said they had subsided over the last few days and he was feeling a lot better, though he felt it might only be a short reprieve for him.

He told me he had felt his 'Earth mission' had gone wrong and that he had been unprepared for the heavy assault from various alien forces beyond the physical. He said now the forum had ended he might go travelling with his family in the near future. They wanted to try to live somewhere else and see if that would be better. He had come over because he wanted to say thank you for being a friend and assisting him with his books. I just told him it was my pleasure and then thanked him for the miraculous energies and journey he had shared.

He just smiled.

Then, as we sat there, I felt a peculiar sensation through my body. There was an energy present which was quickly growing in strength but instead of coming from above as it had before, it swirled around at our feet and then rushed upwards in a wave.

I looked at him and said, "Your energy has changed?"

He looked into my eyes and said, "Can you feel that?"

I told him I was feeling it very strongly as if it was like a vortex pulling my entire being upwards.

It was like some part of Simon was leaving – for me, it is still quite hard to describe.

Again, the energy surged upwards. It did this three times and I could see it as a column of light.

After the third wave we sat quietly for a bit. He said this had been happening sporadically for days now and it was because of this he had decided to dissolve the online forum.

I asked him, "What will you do now?"

"It doesn't really matter now," he replied.

I just took that as a change in his and his family's life direction. I knew he had endured a lot these last years and I wasn't going to push with any questions.

Then he turned to me and said, "Before I forget," and he stood up from his chair and walked into the kitchen to the box on the sink bench saying, "I think this is meant for you." My partner was also in the kitchen as he handed me the box.

I took it from him and opened it. When I looked into it I was a little surprised because in it was what appeared to be a lot of garden litter...twigs and leaves.

I looked at him a little bewildered.

He laughed and said it was from South America and that it was a sacred medicine called Ayahuasca. He told me he had tried to brew it but it hadn't worked. However, he said that after taking it he felt it was meant for me. (This was still a few years before this medicine became better known in the West.)

I said thank you but was quite unsure what to do with it. It would sit in my cupboard for about a year before I was then guided to try it. (In the years to come this would take my life into a complete different tangent but that is another story!)

After that we talked for a little while longer. He then said goodbye to me and my partner and walked out the door. It would be the last time I would see Simon.

17

Hmmm... That Was Strange!

It was a few weeks after that last visit with Simon that I visited a friend's house. Her name was Ann and I had asked her if I could use her computer to quickly check my emails and see if anyone had recently tried to contact me.

She said 'sure' and asked me if I wanted a coffee. I said that would be nice as I sat down in front of her computer, turned it on and proceeded to view my emails. I noticed I had received an email from one of the online members. This was unexpected as I thought the online forum had finished.

When I read it I was completely surprised to read that Simon had possibly committed suicide!

I sat there a little in shock and turned to Ann who was still making me a coffee relaying what the email said. We just sat thinking for a moment as I told her it might be possible. Ann didn't know Simon personally but as Nannup was a small town she knew of him. However, as they were so private, no one really spoke to them much.

Then I said to her, "If that is true I think I should ring Chantelle and see if she is alright or needs anything." Ann agreed. I still had their phone number in my wallet from the time I delivered the gas bottles.

I called their home number and Chantelle answered. I told her about the email and that it stated Simon might have committed suicide. She gave me a strange answer and said, "Is that what they say?"

Then she went on to tell me that everything was fine, Simon included, and said it was just probably a mix up with forum members. I just said "OK, cool," (I had no idea what was happening on the internet forum) and then told her if she or Simon needed anything to just let me know.

She said she would, and we left it at that and said goodbye.

I told Ann who had been listening to my side of the phone conversation that Chantelle had said it was a mix up on the internet. However, we both agreed it was a little weird.

Then I emailed Kirk and Alix who I hadn't contacted for months. I asked them if they had heard any news about Simon explaining what the email had said. They replied saying they hadn't heard anything, telling me they had recently spoken to Simon and he was cool. It seemed like some kind of mix up after all!

Ann said it sounded fine but she would ask around town to see if anyone had heard news about anything related. She never got back to me with anything over the next week so I presumed everything was good.

It was a few months later I found out the family had gone

missing with Tony and that both Kirk and Alix had taken their own lives not long after...

18

OH SHIT!

Western rationality is based on irrational platforms such as the mainstream media. The superficial declarations and false assumptions of reporters who are prompted by selfish motivations and commanded by greedy corporate interests have turned this world into the absurdist theatre it has become. Anyone who has been at ground zero of any newsworthy event or who has been targeted by the media will understand what I'm talking about.

It seems that in the desperate need to get the big headline, networks have gradually effaced any true journalism to bury the truth under superficial platitudes and displays for the self-centred and temporal satisfaction of the viewer. Over the years, I have seen the public feed these illusions because they want to hide from their deeper 'life' responsibilities. Everyone wants a scapegoat and it is easy to point a finger. However, in the end the only realisation the public will have is that their lives have been nothing but a lie.

There was not much time to process all of what had just

happened when one day I went to the local post office to collect my mail and buy a newspaper. On the front cover of the paper was a picture of Simon, Chantelle, Leela and Tony. It had the words 'Family missing' and 'Cult,' in bold print. I just looked at it and thought, 'Oh shit!'

Very quickly the town was abuzz with reporters on the streets interviewing locals. At that time the media was focused on the missing family and did not yet know about Kirk and Alix. I remember going home and telling my partner what was happening.

That night we turned on the television to watch the news.

The term 'cult' was now being used in connection with Simon and the online Gateway forum. Over the next few nights as we watched the news all I could think of was, 'Wow, this is all really messy.' Some people in town were beginning to freak out. There was a small meditation group of mostly elderly ladies that Simon had apparently turned up to one day and they were all scared that they were going to be connected to a death cult. I knew there was no such cult in the town.

I also remember thinking that all this cult talk was foolish and quite premature because no one knew if the family was dead. Knowing the little I did of Chantelle and Simon, I understood this type of talk could possibly drive them to take their lives if they were still alive. It was also reckless because it would stop anyone with any pertinent information from coming forward. I knew I wasn't going to speak to anyone with all the mad media attention.

I watched it all quickly turn into a circus.

As weeks went on, the media would constantly play images

of the family with Tony from a personal home video. They were all saying 'namaste' into a camera and it was quite innocent but the media kept replaying this clip accompanied by sinister music as they continually repeated the words 'death cult' throughout their reporting.

I would sit opened mouthed and amazed as various news stations brought in their 'experts' to comment about the case. It seems our society is full of people sitting on their own intellectual icebergs who love to give their perspectives on everyone and everything. I can only say it was pure dribble.

They had psychologists, cult experts and other intellectuals all commenting and giving their highly 'opinionated facts' about the case.

Seriously, does the mainstream media have a general go-to for dumb-arse?

I can only say this...

If you want a very abstract parody of what is going on in society, keep watching the mainstream media but you must never think that if you watch it you are really being informed!

At that time I was also faced with a dilemma. People were now hearing about the deaths of Kirk and Alix because it was getting out on the internet. I had people who I had known years ago asking me what had happened. These people knew we had all stayed friends but now that the term 'death-cult' had been thrown into the mix some of them were demanding answers and some of them were quite accusative. Most of the answers they desired I could not give because I had barely spoken to them over the last couple of years.

Even Wolfy, who I hadn't heard from in many years, was

asking a few questions that at that time I could not give suitable answers to.

I was in such a strange and surreal position. There was a missing family and two dead friends from Canada who were now connected to some online cult. I had barely any time to process their deaths myself and there was no way I could talk about ETs without looking crazy. How could I explain to anyone about the metaphysical attacks that we had to endure...

It was all so far out of everyone's reality box.

I realised the only thing I could do at that time was just stay silent and let people think what they would.

Most of it wasn't nice. Gossip and rumours spread very quickly and they became a heavy weight I have had to live with.

19

THE POLICE INVESTIGATION

As the reports of the missing family hit the news, the police launched an investigation into the case that would continue to run until the coroner's inquiry a decade later. The police were pleading with the public to help with any information that might lead them to find any member of the missing family.

There was much speculation as to what had happened to them. The general suspicion was that it was probably a murder-suicide or that the family had fled to South America where they were living off grid. Soon family members of the missing and dead were also coming forward on the television and looking for answers. However, as years went by, it seemed they had not turned up anything new. The media eventually became aware of the suicide deaths of Kirk and Alix.

For the most of it, I had been quiet. All my close friends knew about my friendship with Kirk and Alix years before and many of them had read Simon's works but I had very little to offer the police that would interest them. I had no idea what had happened to the family or Tony and I had only heard from Kirk and Alix very casually over the last few years. All I could offer people would be what they would perceive as an obscure rambling on metaphysical attacks from ETs.

Eventually the police, knowing I had known both Kirk and Alix and the family, contacted me for a couple of interviews in the hope I might be able to help them with their inquiries. To be honest, I was reluctant getting involved with the case but by then I knew I was already in it!

I agreed and met with the head detective and another officer who had come down from Perth. They asked me a few questions and asked if I had any information that could help find the missing family. I found the detective a likable man and easy to talk with but had nothing to give him that would assist him. I could see that the case had become somewhat frustrating for him. They told me they had discovered that Simon had been living with a false identity in Australia and that his real name was Gary Fenton. This had cast a very deep suspicion on 'Simon' and it was easy to understand why.

However, it did not surprise me that much. In one of my few meetings with him he had said that after what was a very powerful energetic experience in England, he had been constantly attacked and harassed by certain dark forces and interdimensional entities. Since then he had kept on the move and could not stay in one place for very long as the attacks would begin again.

As you can imagine I could only stay silent about this because there was no point in mentioning it. It wouldn't help the investigation and only just have me sound very strange. However, I could empathise with the detective who I could plainly see just wanted to get on with the investigation and resolve the case.

In the end I had two meetings with the police. The first is described above and the second was in Perth. I had told them previously about the phone call I had made to Chantelle when I had received that strange email. They told me they already had that on record. In essence, I actually had nothing to offer them in regards to the case. I couldn't tell them much about the internet forum because I was not part of the inner group. In fact they were informing me on certain details I had been unaware of. All I remember was thinking that the whole case was a bit strange and confusing, and I could see the police thought the same. After the questioning in Perth the detective thanked me for my help and gave me his card. He told me if I did remember anything that might assist the investigation to call him.

I genuinely wished him well in his enquires. I said to him, "In the end the truth of things is revealed."

I very much believe that!

20

A RE-EVALUATION OF REALITY

I believe humanity is on the verge of a paradigm altering revelation. I learnt through many trials and experiences over years that this world is nothing like what we have been led to believe it is.

The years leading to the deaths of my two friends had me further questioning the world in which we live. The energetic experiences we had shared would only propel me to go further in my quest for the deeper truths that underline our reality. I needed an enlarged context to what I was seeing and experiencing. There were so many unanswered questions with just as many WTF moments!

I was listening to many speakers around the world presenting all sorts of themes and subjects such as aliens, conspiracy, physics, spirituality and metaphysics. So I decided to get in contact with them and spent the next several years travelling, getting to know and quietly working with some of the most diverse and interesting people on the planet. They were activists, whistle-blowers, scientists, intellectuals, alternative media and conspiracy theorists. Some of them are quite famous and others not so well known.

I also used my trips to travel to ancient archaeological sites around the world to study their histories and cultural myths. Along the way I met shamans, initiates and all sorts of esoteric teachers. As you might imagine it was an interesting and sometimes frightening journey. Some of the experiences I had on my travels many people would not believe.

During those years I also spent time online on various spiritual forums and connecting with various spiritual groups. Having gone through a variety of experiences previously and with a deeper insight than most, I had some interesting revelations. A big one was that many of the people I had spoken to over those years had also experienced similar metaphysical attacks or had known others who had gone through the same. Many of them shared their stories and some pointed me to various prominent speakers and writers who had gone public on certain subjects who had then died or who had seemingly lost their minds.

The common theme was that these were some sort of directed inorganic frequency attack, while others had endured more earthly demonic attacks. This was especially the case when there was a sustained gathering of sincere seekers or a person speaking or writing in context to planetary ascension. I realised I was witness to a very real war initiated from different levels of reality trying to stop people from awakening.

Of course this has never been reported in any form of

media. The general public has been conditioned to think that most spiritualists, conspiracy theorists and alternative media are already crazy, often labelling them as tin-foil hat wearers. In a lot of cases I'm not going to deny that is not the case (there are some very 'interesting' people out there but from my experience, that is a reality in all sections of society) but I have come to understand that this is part of a much bigger play. The words 'cult' and 'conspiracy theorist' are sometimes an easy way to invalidate and write off what seems to be a metaphysical play that has been hiding a series of occult attacks that have been happening to particular people around the globe. While some of these events make headlines in the public arena they are written off as psychological case studies for various intellectuals. This is how it is all hidden in plain sight. I am talking of coherent writers, speakers and even well-respected scientists, who have usually at some point publicly challenged the status quo in their fields of research or just the general consensus of formulated opinion.

One of the biggest revelations that came to me was that some of these attacks were coming from certain negatively oriented interdimensional and extraterrestrial beings. In the coming years I would pursue this further...

The reason that I would bring this up here is that certain experiences with Simon had already brought to my awareness that there existed 'other' realities and beings that secretly influence humanity. Some of these intelligences work with a beneficial intent while others are more insidious, and most of humanity is totally unaware of their existence. This had me understand there is a very real enemy that is manipulating the human race.

In relevance to this book, I still believe what was behind Simon was an extraterrestrial being of magnificent scope, attempting to assist humanity. He never hid what was behind him was an ET. His writings and works bore a benevolent signature despite how things might have ended. What this ET being experienced was a sustained attack from other realities that seemed to be part of some greater interdimensional conflict and so it withdrew. What happened after that in terms of the internet group forum I do not know. However, what I do understand is what Kirk and Alix had experienced through those last couple of years had become too much for them.

I have always kept in my heart the beautiful presence I felt in Thailand that had said that everything was going to be alright and was being looked after on other dimensional levels.

That was good enough for me!

21

THE CORONERS INQUEST

Now we fast forward nearly a decade after Simon and his family had gone missing.

The police had subpoenaed me to appear at the coroner's inquest to speak in relation to the case. It was in the town of Busselton, about 50km from the town of Nannup. With no new leads, the case of the missing family was to be declared unsolved.

A couple of friends who I was living with, drove me to the courthouse and we could see news reporters and camera men lined up all around the front entrance. None of the media had spoken to me yet about the case although some had been trying to contact me over the years. I never answered them.

As they didn't know my face, they didn't know who I was which enabled me to quietly slip inside to the courtroom lobby. Once inside I noticed several people already there in connection to the case who I had seen on the news. Some were Tony's family. I had never actually met them before.

As I sat there waiting for the proceedings to start I realised some of the reporters had noticed me and were going through the court list to find out who I was. Others, having obtained my name, were going through my Facebook page to get a rundown on who I was. As most of the media had not much to go on throughout the entire case, they were desperate to glean any new information they could. I realised their attention was now focused on me and what I had to say. It all felt quite predatory.

It is here I would like to share some of the tactics used by some of the large television network reporters. Most of them were females aged in their mid-twenties to mid-thirties. They all dressed very similar and looked sort of cloned. A few of them came straight up to me very flirtatiously and asked for an interview after the court hearing. I could see none of them really cared that I had lost some close friends or gave a crap about what damage they were potentially doing to people's lives. It was like they were blowing kisses only to probably stab me in the back with their pens later.

Anything to get the story eh?

All of it was gross!

Anyway, we were then all called into the courtroom.

I don't know if anyone reading this has actually had to sit through any courtroom proceeding but I have to say this; it is very long-winded and boring. Time goes very slowly. I don't want to bore you with any details that are not relevant to this book so I won't say much except throughout the hearing no one offered up anything that hadn't been said before.

After a few hours and a couple of testimonies, I was

MEMOIRS OF A 'DEATH CULT'

eventually called to the stand. I looked around. The head detective was sitting close by and the coroner sat on the right beside the witness stand.

Most of the reporters were sitting in one line with their pens and note pads out.

On the stand I was asked about my friendship with Kirk and Alix and how we met. I was asked about how I met Simon's family and if I knew of the online group forum. I told them I knew about it but wasn't an inner group member.

As you can understand there was no way I could relate anything like I have shared in this book. If I had tried, it would have turned the entire thing into a spectacle and made it much worse for everyone. The police were only interested in the facts that would resolve the case and find the missing family. I could not share anything that would help in these matters so I just stayed silent about these other things.

After a series of questions the coroner asked if I considered Simon a friend.

When I said YES all the reporters simultaneously started to scribble in their notepads.

I knew by saying this I was going to be targeted by the media. You see, throughout this entire case everyone was demonising Simon, or if they knew him were thoroughly distancing their selves from him. For years the word 'cult' had been thrown around, and in all the heartbreak and confusion surrounding the case you had to be against Simon otherwise you would instantly be associated with being part of something sinister. This is people's 'justifiable' emotive irrationality!

From that moment, my life would change.

I could see no one cared that I had actually only met with Simon a handful of times over the course of seven years. We had exchanged emails at various times but I was not part of anything evil. If anything it had been the opposite. In each contact he had always been genuine and friendly even if it was sometimes a bewildering experience.

However, this did not matter to anyone because now that I had called him a friend, my name and everything I would say from that moment on would be mud to the public. This was because throughout all the years of investigation the media had never had anyone to tangibly vilify because Simon was missing and no one else was talking much. Now they finally had someone to actually bite into.

I watched the row of reporters become a row of salivating hell hounds.

After my testimony had finished the coroner said there would be a short recess. I was finished so I had no real need to go back into the court and I was relieved it was done. However, I could see that many of the reporters were now eyeing me off and I had no wish to walk outside into crazy.

It was then one of the reporters who had already approached me before the hearing, walked up as everyone was leaving the room. She asked for a personal interview outside but as I looked into her eyes she looked very sharky. I politely declined.

So then she decided to get harsh with me and actually told me, that she would be "getting an interview with me outside whether I liked it or not."

I asked her how she thought she was going to do that and

she just replied very condescendingly, "We can make you do what we want."

I won't say here which channel she worked for.

She left to go outside and wait for me.

I was quite angered by these words so I turned around and walked up to the head detective and asked if there was another way out the courtroom. As I said before, he was a nice man and I think he could tell what was about to happen to me. I wasn't under suspicion for anything so he just directed me out a back door of the courtroom. I remain really appreciative to him for that!

Walking onto the street a couple of hundred metres up from where the media had gathered waiting for me I breathed a sigh of relief. I then walked away, leaving the madness behind me.

22

BRANDED!

Question: Aren't you that guy who was part of some death cult?

Answer: No dickhead, if I was would I be here talking with you now?

The next day after the coroner's inquest I turned on my computer to read the news. On the main page of the world news was my picture and I was quoted on my statements in regards to the case. I knew from that day onwards I would always be associated publicly with the term 'death cult.'

I understood that no matter what I did or said from then on would simply be invalidated in the public arena. I had already been through enough public trashing for several years because I had been working in the 'alternative media' (when it still had integrity.) The words 'conspiracy theorist' had been thrown at me a lot but now that I had been caught up in this series of events I was truly an outcast.

It wouldn't matter if I knew nothing about the missing family or wasn't involved in the death of my friends. I would wear a social conviction through association. I had been digitally branded which meant in this current world it would be very hard to make a living.

So I took off with a few friends to live in the more isolated and quieter places of Western Australia.

I'm sure that as you read this you might punch my name into your computer and read the articles relating to this case. You might possibly say that most of these articles don't post me in a bad light. But as I said at the beginning of this book, we live in a courtroom of public opinion and the facts do not matter much there. Fear and gossip are what sentences you.

The word 'cult', or even worse 'death cult', instantly relegates anyone associated with it as being part of something suspicious or sinister. Its label will have you instantly invalidated in people's minds. The fact is I have not and will never condone suicide.

I want people reading this book to understand that in no way is this book an attempt for some kind of reconciliation or re-acceptance by the world ego. Personally, I don't care what you think and I'm quite happy living in the remoter parts of Australia.

However, over the last decades I have watched this world gradually become stranger and more dystopian.

What I want you to do is ask why?

I know many people might think this statement is amusing

by some guy trying to tell people that there are aliens manipulating the human race. To this, all I can say is that I'm trying to point out that there may be deeper causes and explanations to the madness you are now witnessing in the world. As I observe our global society going through a tremendous change, I see the necessity of sharing this story.

So now you have been warned. I have been doing my best for decades to bring all this to greater public awareness and have put my neck out many times in doing so. So don't come crying to me in the future, especially while today, you harass and downplay real alternative media, conspiracy theorists and people like myself who have been trying to share these subjects with you. If you don't wake up and consider these subjects a little deeper I can assure you will all soon be in for some very hard cosmic lessons. There is a reason why so many people are coming out and talking about such experiences.

23

THE STORY WITHIN THE STORY

At the beginning of this book I said that there was a deeper tale than just that of a missing family and the death of a few close friends. While the mystery of the missing family and the suicides of Kirk and Alix are a tragedy, their deaths are the only things that seem to be of importance to the mainstream media. By them we are given the simplistic explanation of a death cult which seems to wrap everything up quite neatly in the eyes of the public.

However, the real travesty is that the true story has been buried.

As unbelievable as it will be to many people, the real story is in fact about contact with an extra-terrestrial entity from much higher dimensions of our universal reality and its attempt to reach humanity through a personality called Simon. This event was witnessed and engaged by a large assortment of people from around the world via the Gateway forum.

However, all of this also came with the disturbing revelation of a hostile group of alien antagonists that have been hiding themselves in other dimensional layers of reality, that have secretly attacked anyone around the globe who have come close to discovering or revealing the reality of their existence. This is the true story that provides a real context as to what happened over those years.

As I come to the end of this small book I realise there are so many more events and happenings I could have shared with the reader. However, these things are not pertinent to the basic themes that are being conveyed in this book. What I have tried to share with the reader is that there are many events happening all around them that are defined from far beyond their own self-centred versions and perceptions of reality.

Having journeyed around this planet questing for deeper knowledge and being witness to many things beyond what is today considered plausible by our current society, I can say that one of the greatest mistakes people make is to assume that how they live and experience their lives is how everyone else experiences reality. You would be very surprised to learn what is really going on 'out there'. People live in a façade, a consensus reality that they have been led to believe is real.

However, there are many diverse energetic realities that overlap your own little versions of time- space. There are beings that exist in other consciousness spectrums. Have you ever thought that perhaps some of these beings are trying to keep you locked down in this construct of reality so that you remain unaware of their hidden control over you?

This story did not finish with the events that transpired

in this book. All that happened in these pages were just a small stepping stone that began this writer's greater journey. Eventually this would lead the writer through levels of divine initiation and experiential contact with an assortment of extraterrestrial beings and intelligences. This included a few run-ins with those of a more hostile alien disposition. These beings do exist and are influencing the world from many levels of your reality.

However, in respect to these things I would ask the reader to refrain from any judgements about these matters until they have read some of my other writings where there is a much better contextual framework. There was only so much that could be written within the confines of this short work.

24

PRE-EMPTIVE CONSIDERATIONS

Because of the large amount of attention focused on this case from around the world, I need to say a few things in regards to the possibility of attacks from sources such as the mainstream media and general academia. Knowing very well their disposition to trash these subjects as well as the person relating them, I've had to pre-emptively consider and tackle some of those more common accusations that could be thrown at me. (I'm sure in reading this book that many people have now upgraded my associative 'cult' label to 'ALIEN DEATH CULT' status!)

After a discussion with a few of my friends I have decided the most important are…

1. **There would be certain people inclined to believe that I have made this story completely up in some sad attempt to rationalise or cope with the deaths and disappearance of people around me.**

To this I would say that I have kept many emails sent by those involved throughout those years. In these emails Kirk, Alix and others related to the online forum talk about the attacks they endured, their metaphysical insights, as well as their more extraordinary contacts with Simon. These are a genuine compilation and record of those events as they happened years ago.

I will give an example of this...

A few years after the family went missing I contacted one of the internet inner group forum members. Her name was Sandra and I asked her a few questions to get a bit more clarity in regards to what happened in those last couple of years on the forum. I related a couple of my experiences with Simon and here is what she replied with...

If this is helpful: From the moment I met Si, he mostly communicated with an aspect through him that he called "the Other". It departed from him in June 2003 - about the time the group experienced a sudden growth spurt that dramatically re-arranged its "matrix" (so to say). The Other was a direct representative of Christ. I do not know why it withdrew, only that Si's vehicles were utterly exhausted. And that afterwards, there were many, many changes ultimately leading to external group dissolution.

So you can clearly see that this writer is not making this up but simply pointing out that there is a genuine story within a story that goes well beyond what has been covered by the media. It also explains why there was so much secrecy in regards to witnesses coming forward in relation to the case.

2. **Writing this book I am seeking to profit or capitalise from this tragic event.**

The only reason I decided to write this book was from an inner prompting after so many years of being continually contacted by various journalists and writers who for their own selfish motives desired only to put their spin on things.

You can imagine that having sat with this information for over two decades and having watched various current affairs shows, internet news and newspapers regurgitate the same rubbish year after year, I was tired of it. Having also been a witness to these events personally, I was also compelled by a deeper urge to write this book to clean up the rather morbid and growing cluster of thought-forms that had gathered around the entire affair.

I will also be quite direct here –

If I did gain any money from writing this book, what is it to you?

I will ask you again, do you actually understand what it is like to be publicly associated with a so called death cult?

No, you don't!

When you have been labelled in the said manner, try to make any sort of basic living and come tell me how you have done it! I have been writing books for over thirty years to a very limited audience. In all probability this book will probably get buried as many such books are buried because it deals with topics that most of the public cannot respectfully deal with.

In saying that, I would now like to address all those who might have a problem with these subjects.

Having travelled around the globe all my life and worked with some of the most unique and amazing people, sharing their deep insight and experiencing many strange things, I am telling you there is a collective recognition and dawning coming to you all soon, whether you like it or not.

This revelation is that we are not alone and never have been. I am talking in relevance to more highly advanced extra-terrestrial species that have been interacting with our race over untold millennia. Who are even today influencing many facets of human society from levels of reality that aren't usually considered in today's academic framework.

Now you can come at me with all your anecdotes, psychological assessments and lineal perceptions but guess what?

'Contact' has been happening everywhere.

The question many of you academics and scientists should be asking is why have you been unable to recognise that this phenomena has been happening to people throughout the world?

Here is some advice...

The ego-mind by itself is a very poor tool to contextualise and explore the true multi-dimensional nature of our universe. Being unable to validate anything beyond their self-relative experiences and belief structures, mental types usually have a need to define or contain all experience into their own limited versions of attainable self-reference.

In their assessments of reality, most academics have mistakenly bypassed or invalidated their own multi-dimensional capability by not recognising the true potentiality of the bio-energetic, human organism.

Would you also consider that the current tendency towards materialism that is being demonstrated by our scientific community might be nothing but a by-product of an inherent energetic imbalance that has out pictured through a progressive overreliance on the intellect? This overreliance on the ego-mind has now become the lamentable obstruction to our species' growth because it stops us from realising our essential spiritual nature. Though many would deny it, as a cultured habituation it is underlined by nothing more than a survivalist mentality that stems from a deep fear of invalidation.

Perhaps this is why we see so much sophistic pageantry in our learning institutions today?

What I'm trying to say is that the recognition of contact and sustained interaction with an extraterrestrial species and/or civilisation might be subconsciously invalidated or circumvented by much of our present intellectual community because such contact would potentially disqualify much of what they have engineered as their collective 'perceptional base' in explaining 'reality'.

However, if this is the hidden reason behind their refutations then this is simply collective egotism.

I would also point out the possibility that it is also this very fear that may have been exploited by certain despotic forces to intentionally culture a progressive 'over-mentalisation of everything' within our modern academia. This is because it keeps people from recognising what should be obvious and apparent.

With a little exploration and inquiry it's not hard to gather an overwhelming amount of evidence as to extraterrestrial realities presently interacting with our world. Our governments are very aware of what has been happening but for their own reasons have been withholding an incredible amount of information.

Over the years I have personally identified and engaged with several ET species. You just have to learn the true 'science' of contact!

What's been holding you back?

Are you waiting for the media to officially inform you?

Good luck with that!

25

FINAL WORDS

Decades ago if someone had said that in the future I would be living in the remote parts of Western Australia having been rejected by society because of my involvement with an international death cult and writing about my own personal liaisons and experiences with an extraterrestrial species, I would have told them to put down their crack pipe.

But now, here we are...

However, as I contemplate the many weird events that have woven themselves into the unique tapestry of my strange little life I can only be very grateful to God for every single one of them. There have been so many trials and dangers but also so much genuine Divine Grace throughout it all, that I just want to tell readers how thankful I am. I have always considered those energies that were shared by Simon as sacred.

If I would share anything with people in these last paragraphs, it is this; I know that many of you are going through difficult times right now. The world is changing swiftly and society seems to have gone on some weird bender but this is because many of you continue to hold onto a dying paradigm that cannot give you any real context as to what is truly happening in the world at this time. You need to let go of all of your expectations, assumptions and demands of life otherwise things are only going to get stranger. Please, take a step back to reconsider your lives and understand what it means to really live. You can recreate yourselves. Life can be a beautiful and sacred experience but that depends on you and what you do with it.

I know that many of your children have been trying to tell you this for years in their own unique ways. Over the last decades many of them have been awakening and finding a deeper connection to Mother Earth. They have been rediscovering the world and working with their true spiritual nature though you still haven't heard them. They have been trying to warn what you will lose if you continue down your present pathways. Kirk and Alix years ago tried to share their otherworldly experiences and deep insights but they were not listened to or taken seriously. I know that is what killed them even if it was by their own hands.

I understand that contemplations on alien realities manipulating the human race is scary to many people but to ignore it is potentially far worse. With so much information coming into the public arena by various sources it's all heading to a collective realisation whether you want it to or not.

I said at the very beginning of this book that I have written it in the temperament and vernacular of a younger version of myself who was just setting out to discover the deeper truths of Life. In my written work over recent years I have become more disciplined in respect to the written word. However, while writing this work and 'letting loose' in regards to its colloquial delivery, I came to my own moment of healing and rediscovery – that little piece of myself that became splintered decades ago when so much negative energy was being incessantly thrown at me. It was like an aspect of my voice was stolen from me back then and has now been returned and re-integrated.

So now I come to address the corporate mainstream media...

Over the years I have watched you peddle so much fear and confusion around the world. You have shown yourselves to be one of the most vile and despicable forces on the face of the Earth at this time. Do you not even think about the karmic ramifications of what you are doing?

We all can now see who and what you really serve.

All you loathsome and selfish sell-outs who make up the collective body of our current global media, you are truly murderers *en masse* and yet have the nerve to associate me with a death cult!

All I will say to you is have a good look in a mirror and then take these writings and go shove them up your bottom.

Writing that felt good!

I know that many of them will be reading this book!

My name is Warren Sunkar and these are my memoirs of a 'Death Cult.'

www.ingramcontent.com/pod-product-compliance
Lightning Source LLC
Chambersburg PA
CBHW070435010526
44118CB00014B/2052